HEAVEN AND MIRTH®

John the Baptist
Wet & Wild

AND
OTHER BIBLE STORIES TO TICKLE YOUR SOUL

by Mike Thaler

Illustrated by Dennis Adler

*Equipping Kids
for Life*

A Faith Parenting Guide can be found on page 32.

For Kathleen Campbell Wright
Spreading the Good News with love
Mike

Faith Kids® is an imprint of
Cook Communications Ministries, Colorado Springs, CO 80918
Cook Communications, Paris, Ontario
Kingsway Communications, Eastbourne, England

JOHN THE BAPTIST: WET & WILD
© 2001 by Mike Thaler for text and Dennis Adler for illustrations

Faith Kids® is a registered trademark of Cook Communications Ministries.

HEAVEN AND MIRTH® is a registered trademark of Mike Thaler.

Published in association with the literary agency of Alive Communications, Inc.,
7680 Goddard St., Suite 200, Colorado Springs, CO 80920.

Edited by Jeannie Harmon
Designed by Clyde Van Cleve

First printing, 2001
Printed in Singapore
05 04 30 02 01   5 4 3 2 1

ISBN 0-78143-513-7

Letter from the Author

Taking this opportunity, I would like to share with you how this book came about. Born sixty-two years ago, I have been a secular children's book author most of my life. I was also content to have a fast-food relationship with God from the drive-by window. At the age of sixty, I came into the banquet by inviting Jesus Christ into my heart. Since then my life has been a glorious feast. These stories are part of that celebration.

One night I sat and watched a sincere grandfather trying to read Bible stories to his squirming grandchildren. I asked him, "Aren't there any humorous retellings of Bible stories that are vivid and alive for kids?" He rolled his eyes and said, "This is it." The kids rolled their eyes, too.

This made me sad, for the Bible is the most exciting, valuable, and alive book I know—as is its Author. So I went into my room, with this in mind, and wrote "Noah's Rainbow."

Since then God has anointed me with sixty stories that fire my imagination and light up my heart. They are stories which, I hope, are filled with the joy, love, and spirit of the Lord.

Mike Thaler
West Linn 1998

Nuggets from Goldie the miner prophet:
"It's Never Too Late to Eat Right."

Author's Note

I have conscientiously tried to follow each story in word and spirit as found in the Bible. But in some cases, for the sake of storytelling, I have taken minor liberties and added small details. I pray for your understanding in these instances.

4

John the Baptist
Wet & Wild

JOHN THE BAPTIST WAS WILD
even before he was born.
When he first met Jesus
in the womb next door,
he started jumping up and down.

"Wow!" said Elizabeth to Mary.
"My baby is sure glad to meet
your baby!"

John's father, Zechariah,
  was a high priest,
  and John grew up in a repent house.★

When John was fifteen,
  he hit the road for God,
  jumping up and down,
  and proclaiming
  the coming of the Messiah.

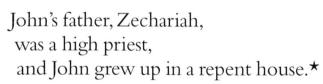

He was not your typical evangelist.
He never cut or combed his hair.

★The floor above the penthouse.

He lived in the desert
and wore a rough camel skin tunic,
luckily one without a hump.
And he would bug people
by eating locusts dipped in honey.
Crunch!

He'd bug them further
by jumping up and down
and calling them vipers!

"Repent!" he shouted,
"for the Messiah
is coming."

Then he'd throw them
in the water.
There was very little
in the way of
entertainment
in those days,
so many people
came to see him.

But the best day of his life was when
the Messiah came to see him.

"Will you baptize Me?" asked Jesus.

"Lamb of God,
I'm not even worthy
to snap the Velcro
on Your sneakers.
You baptize me."

"No," smiled Jesus,
"you baptize Me."

"I'll baptize You,
if you baptize me."

"Deal," said Jesus.

So John baptized Him.
And when Jesus came
out of the water,
the heavens
opened up
and the Holy Spirit
descended,
and God said,
"This is My son, whom I love,
with Him I am well pleased.

So dry Your hair,
or You'll catch a cold."

After that day
John got even wilder.
He started writing irate letters
to King Herod
telling him to repent of his wicked ways,
like marrying his brother's wife.
Herod didn't take kindly
to John's advice
and threw him in the slammer.

Herod's wife, Herodias, was even more ticked off.
And at Herod's birthday party her daughter, Salome,
did such a terrific dance that the king offered her
anything she wanted.

At her mom's prompting, she asked for the head
of John the Baptist.

The king tried to dissuade her,
    "Wouldn't you rather
        have a sports chariot
            or new ballet shoes?"

But she insisted
and a promise is a promise.
So John, who was always far out,
finally lost his head completely.
His disciples came and buried the rest of him.
On his body stone,
(they couldn't put up a headstone)
they wrote:

JOHN THE BAPTIST

HE SERVED GOD

FROM WOMB

TO TOMB!

THE END

Nuggets from Goldie, the miner prophet:
"God is all that really matters, even with your heads on platters."

For the real story, read Matthew 3 and Mark 6:14–29.

The Temptation of Christ
Not Likely!

THE HOLY SPIRIT LANDED ON JESUS,
and led Him into the desert to be tempted by the devil,
who ran a frozen yogurt stand.
He also served other things
like devil dogs,
deviled eggs, and
devil's food cake.
But Jesus didn't
touch a thing.
In fact, he fasted
for forty days.

"Well," said the devil,
"if you're not going
to order anything,
turn these rocks into tennis shoes."

13

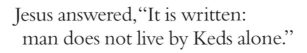

Jesus answered, "It is written:
man does not live by Keds alone."

Then the devil took Jesus to a very high place.
"If You're the Son of God, jump off."

But Jesus was not trying to make an impression,
so He answered, "Don't put the Lord your God
to a test, or a quiz."

Then the devil took Jesus
to the top of the Empire State Building.

"This could all be yours, kid.
I got connections
in publishing
and Hollywood,
and I would be
your soul agent, for only 50%."

"Beat it, devil, the Lord God
gets 100% of My soul."

"Curses," said the devil.
"I'll go find guys
I can make deals with.
Here's my card just in case
you change you mind."

"Not likely," said Jesus,
tearing up the card.
And angels descended
bringing Him
Kool Aid and pizza,
for God was proud
of His son!

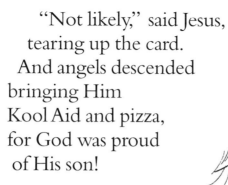

THE END

Nuggets from Goldie, the miner prophet:
"Satan tries like the devil to win you over."

For the real story, read Matthew 4:1–11.

15

Paul in Ephesus
Idol Threats

Paul entered Ephesus and asked believers if they had received the Holy Spirit.

"We have school spirit," they answered.

"Wrong one," said Paul, and he laid hands on them and they became filled with the Holy Spirit.

"Wow!" they said, "this beats school spirit by a mile!"

Word got around and many came to hear about the power of God. Even Paul's laundry could cure the sick and drive out the demons.

Some non-Christians even started
using the name of Jesus
to drive out demons.
   Until one day a demon called their bluff,
   and had a *demon-stration*.

   "I know the power of Jesus,"
    said the demon,
       "and I know the power of Paul.
        But who the heck are you?"
          He roared and fell upon them,
            beat them, and sent them
              all home crying.

When people heard about this,
   they decided to stop messing around
and get serious about Jesus.
   Wizards turned in their wands,
witches turned in their brooms,
and warlocks turned in
their warkeys.
They confessed their sins
and became filled
   with the Holy Spirit.

As more and more people
   turned away from false gods,
   THE FALSE GOD
   MAKERS GUILD
      got panicky.

"My business is off 50%
   since Paul came to town.
      I haven't sold a gold cow in weeks."

"I haven't sold a silver Artemis★ in months."

★pronounced Arty-mess

"I haven't sold a tin chicken all year."

They became very angry and grabbed two of Paul's helpers.

"Artemis is the best!" they all shouted.

When the disciples tried to explain about Jesus, the crowd started singing "For She's a Jolly Good Goddess."

Things were getting out of hand, when the city clerk stood up.

"Listen guys, we know our gods are the best, so cool it. Business will pick up around Christmas.

Philip and the Ethiopian
Hitch-High-King

NOW AN ANGEL OF THE LORD told Philip, "Go south, young man." So he hit the road.

Along the way he ran across a unique eunuch who was treasurer for Candace, Queen of Ethiopia. He had gone to Jerusalem to worship, and on his way home he stopped to read a book.

The angel told Philip to talk to him.
"Hi, what are you reading?"

"Why, I'm reading the book of Isaiah.
It's #1 on the *Times* bestseller list."

"Is it good?" asked Philip

"I don't know, I don't understand it,"
answered the eunuch, scratching his turban.

"Would you like me to explain it?
I saw the movie."

"Sure," said the eunuch,
"Hop in my chariot and I'll give you a lift."

Then he read Philip the part out loud
about "a quiet lamb
who died without a peep."

"Who is the prophet talking about?"
asked the eunuch.

"Well, I'll tell you, Nick,
he's talking about Jesus Christ,
our Lord and Savior."

Philip went on
and told him the good news,
and when they passed a rest stop
with a pond, the eunuch said,
"Let's pull over
and get some coffee,
a donut, and a baptism."

So Philip and the eunuch
got out of the chariot
and jumped into the pond,
where Philip baptized him.
When they came out
of the water,
an angel suddenly
snatched Philip away.

The eunuch was so happy
he didn't even notice
that Philip was gone,
and he went into the men's room
to dry himself off
with the electric hand dryer.

Philip showed up later
in other towns
preaching the gospel.

The eunuch,
even though it took him
a long time to get dry,
stayed happy,
for at last he understood the book,
and had found
the true treasure.

THE END

Nuggets from Goldie, the miner prophet:
"Sometimes you can be smart and be all wet at the same time."

For the real story, read Acts 8:26–40.

The Wise and Foolish Builders

Build by the Code

BESIDES BEING THE SON OF GOD,
the King of kings, and the Prince of peace,
Jesus was also a good carpenter.
Being one,
He knew how to build.

One day after watching "God's
Home Improvement" show
on TV,
He went out
and spoke to the people
of Capernaum.

"When you call Me Lord,
 but don't do what I say,
  you are like a man building his house
   on chocolate pudding.

The first flood will wash it away.

But if you hear Me, and follow My words,
 you are like a man building his house on bedrock.
  And no matter how strong the flood,

his house will stand.

In other words, if you don't
practice what I preach,
it's like building
sand castles at the beach.
But if you come to the altar,
it's like building on
Gibraltar."

Then He *hammered*
home the point,
and *drilled* them,
till they finally *saw* it.

THE END

Nuggets from Goldie, the miner prophet:
"If you want a standing foundation, give God a standing ovation!"

For the real story, read Luke 7:46-49.

HEAVEN AND MIRTH®

John the Baptist
Wet & Wild

Age: 6 and up

Life Issue:
Having faith in God and His Word will help us make right choices.

Spiritual Building Block:
Faith

Learning Styles
Help your child learn about faith in the following ways:

Sight: If your child has a children's version of the Bible, locate and read the story about Paul. (The reference is given at the end of the story.) How did Paul show faith in God? How did God help him?

Sound: Faith is not easy to measure. It is the evidence of things we believe about God but can't see. Talk to your child about what things you believe about God (He is always with us; He will protect us; He will provide for our needs, etc.). Make a list and have your child tape it to the refrigerator.

Touch: Try this experiment: At the beach or in a sandbox at home, have your child place a rock flat enough to support a play house. Then have him or her build a small house out of Legos. Build a small mound of sand and place one house on the top. Place the other house on the rock. With a hose or bucket of water, thoroughly wet the area with water. What happens to the house on the sand? to the house on the rock? What did Jesus mean when He said that we should build our house upon the rock?